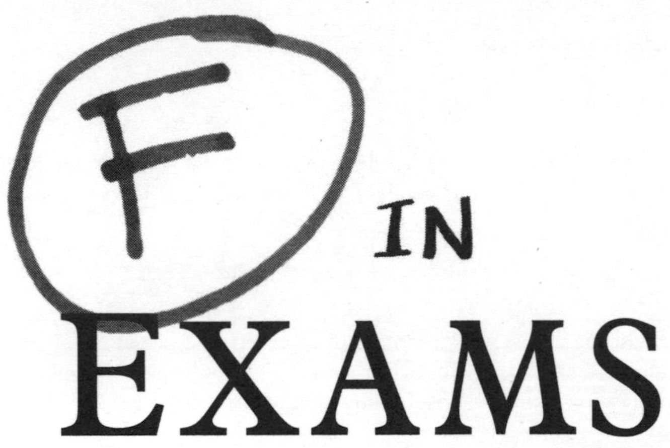
F
IN
EXAMS

F IN EXAMS (2018)

Summersdale Publishers Ltd
46 West Street
Chichester
West Sussex
PO19 1RP
UK

www.summersdale.com

Printed and bound by CPI Group (UK) Ltd, Croydon, CR0 4YY

ISBN: 978-1-78685-208-3

EXAMS

EVEN MORE of the Best Test Paper Blunders

Richard Benson

Contents

Introduction

Class is back in F-in session! Or rather, *F in Exams* is back with the most outrageous, defiant and downright mystifying test paper answers ever penned, collected here for your amusement. The subjects might change, the exam questions might get harder (or easier, depending on which reports you believe) but nothing manages to curb the enthusiasm of those ingenious students who prefer to think outside of the box, or even on another page, when it comes to devising their answers.

Subject: Biology

In the human digestive system, what is the function of bile?

It helps to break down farts.

A diet that consists of unhealthy foods can promote obesity. Give two examples of components that might cause obesity:

One large portion of dessert.

A second large portion of dessert.

Biology

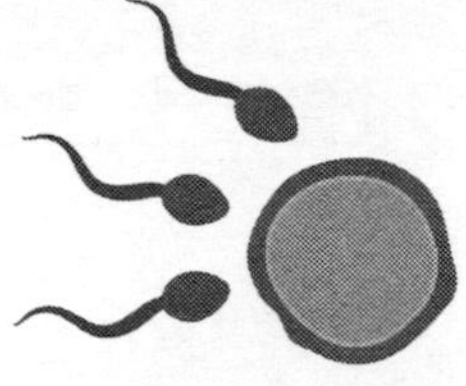

Describe the biological process illustrated above.

Tadpole football.

Puberty results in changes in the body for males and females. Give two examples of changes in males:

Boys grow annoying wispy moustaches.

Girls start keeping their bedroom doors shut during the daytime.

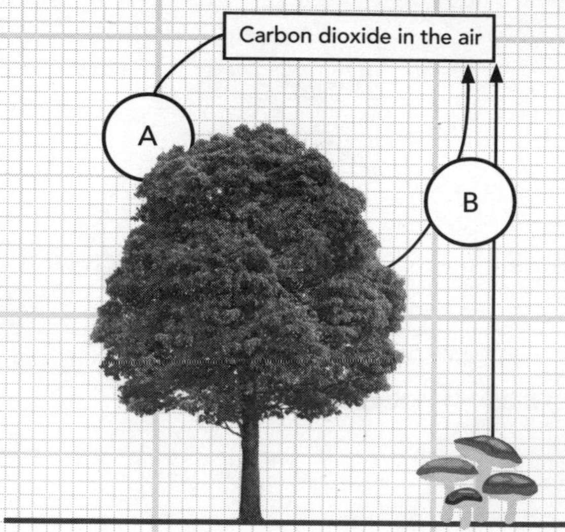

The diagram above shows part of the carbon cycle. Name the processes occurring at points A and B.

Process A

Process B

Biology

Hormones can affect the functions of various organs. Complete the following sentence:
Hormones given to women to stimulate the release of eggs are called ......Laxative............drugs

At birth, the personal traits of identical twins will be the same in a number of ways, but later in life some of their traits might be different. Give two reasons as to why their traits might be different in later life:

They might get annoyed at being confused by strangers, so they would wear different colours to show they are different.

One could turn out to be an evil twin.

By 1820, Russian flu killed 1 million people worldwide. By 1920, Spanish flu had killed 80 million people worldwide.
Give one reason why Spanish flu killed more people.

more people go on holiday to Spain than to Russia.

Sulphur dioxide in the air can negatively affect the development of lichen in urban areas. Give one potential source of sulphur dioxide.

Eggy farts.

Biology

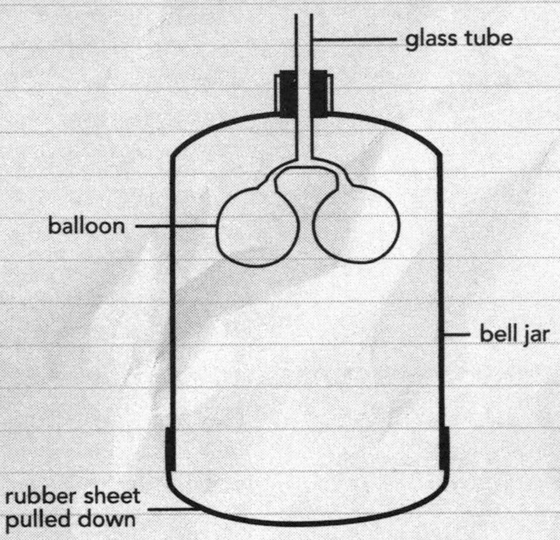

The diagram above is a model of the human respiratory system. Name the parts of the system that are represented by the tube and the rubber sheet.

Urethra

Buttocks

The illustration above shows a desert-dwelling rodent known as a jerboa. Give one example of how its biological features might help it avoid predators in its natural environment.

With the right trainer, it could evolve into its next form and win more Pokébattles.

Complete the following sentence:
Waste converted into compost by organisms is called...........

Worm Poo

Subject: Chemistry

Russian scientist Mendeleev created the first periodic table, consisting of 60 elements. He left gaps in the table – explain why.

for colouring in.

Diamond is made up of carbon. Name a gas that is produced when carbon reacts with oxygen.

CARBOXYGEN

Petrol is one useful product that can be refined from a substance containing a mixture of hydrocarbons. What is this substance?

Rude oil

Farmers often use ammonium salts to replace lost nitrogen in soil. What is this process commonly known as?

Fartilisation

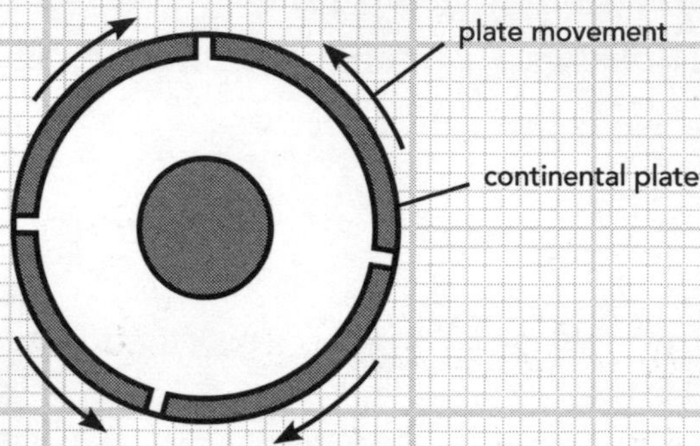

Wegener's hypothesis regarding plate tectonics suggests that over time continents move a few centimetres per year. Complete the following statements:

Inside the earth Digestive processes release energy. This energy heats up the material in the earth's Colon, producing convection currents.

Aluminium is commonly used to make drinks cans. Give two reasons why we should recycle aluminium cans:

Because it says to on the can.

So as not to discriminate between the different types of can.

Water needs to be processed to remove any harmful bacteria before it can be consumed. Describe one other way water can be made safe for consumption.

Buy it in a bottle from a shop.

A bottle of liquid in the laboratory shows the symbol above. What does it mean?

Beware of pirates.

Iron and sulphur are two elements found in the periodic table. What is the name of the compound formed when iron reacts with sulphur?

Sulphurion.

Professional athletes are regularly tested for the use of performance-enhancing drugs, often by giving a blood sample. When a blood sample is taken it is often split into two portions. Each portion is tested at a different laboratory. Why is this important?

So the samples have time to get switched, so the athlete doesn't get ~~[illegible]~~ caught

To combat air pollution, hydrogen-powered cars have been developed. Explain why hydrogen can be considered to be cleaner than petrol.

There is hydrogen in water; we use water to wash ourselves. Therefore, hydrogen is cleaner than petrol.

Magnesium chloride is a white crystalline solid at room temperature with a melting point of 714°C. State two other physical properties of magnesium chloride:

It's Shiny

It's Magnetic

Subject: Physics

Explain the formula used to calculate the density of a substance.

THICKNESS + HARDNESS = DENSITY

Give one safety feature of a modern car which might reduce the injuries to passengers if involved in a road traffic accident.

Softer Seats.

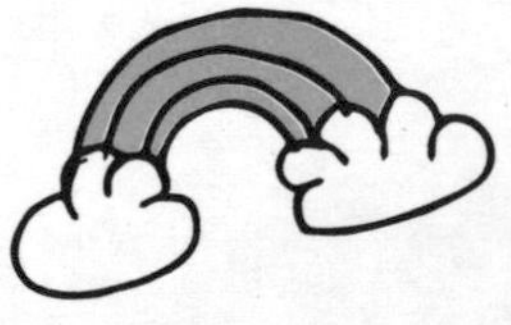

Physics

The diagram shows how electricity is distributed from a power station to consumers.

Fill in the missing label on the diagram.

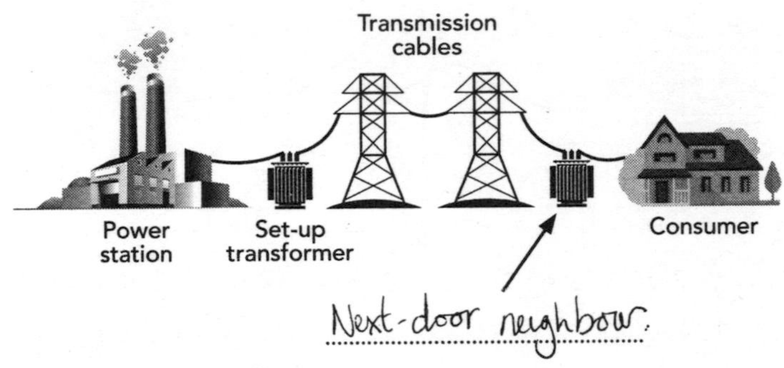

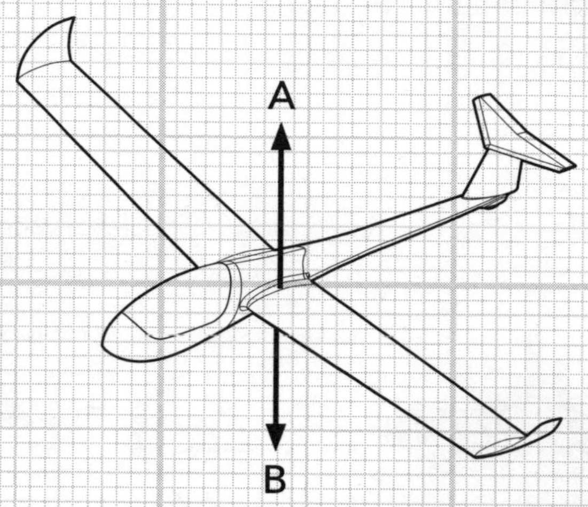

The illustration below shows forces A and B acting on the glider when in flight. What is force B?

The whells

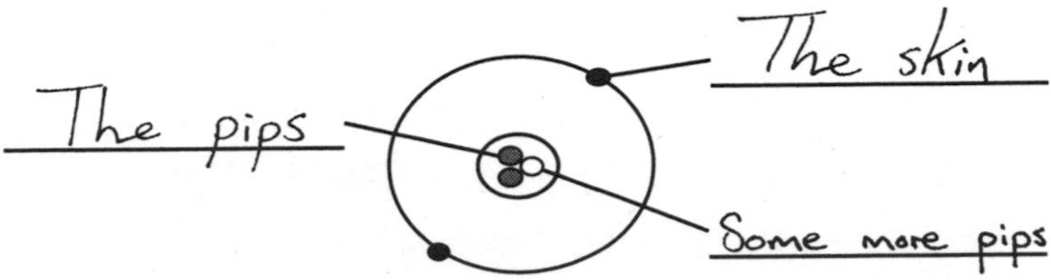

The diagram above shows a neutral atom in the chemical element helium. Label the particles correctly.

Describe two ways in which using nuclear power stations to generate electricity is better than using gas-fired power stations:

You don't have to muck around with that sparky lighter thing.

Gas smells.

Radio waves, microwaves, infrared and visible light are all parts of the electromagnetic spectrum that are used for communication.
State one property that they all have in common.

They are all used in James Bond films.

Figure 3 shows a racing car. Give one feature that will prevent the car from rolling over during a race.

The track does not have any ramps, loops or speed bumps.

Explain what you understand by the term 'ionising radiation'?

When your mum irons your clothes and they become radiated/hot like radiators.

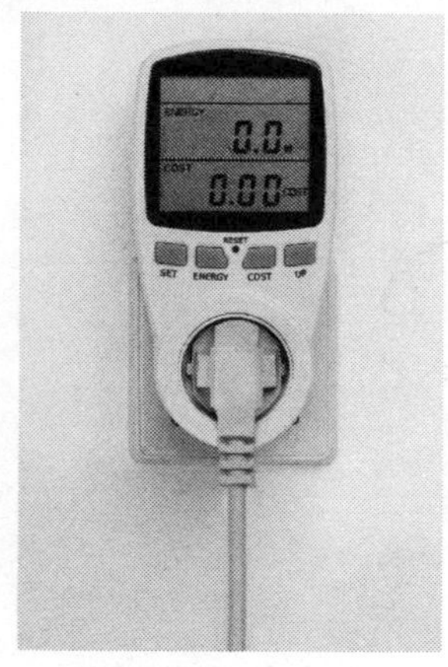

What best describes the object in the image above?

iPod Classic

Subject: ....Drama....

Consider the live performance of William Shakespeare's *Hamlet* you experienced during your course. Give details of the vocal and physical skills demonstrated by one or more of the performers.

One of the actors had a twitch in his left eye.
Hamlet's bum looked nice in tights, and it made a swishing sound as he walked on stage.

Give an example of a time you experienced effective use of lighting in a live stage performance.

When the play ended, they switched on the lights in the theatre so we could see where the exit was

Sketch a costume idea for one of the characters in Sean O'Casey's *Juno and The Paycock.*

Describe two of the main themes in Samuel Beckett's *Waiting for Godot*:

Waiting

Godot

Comedy and tragedy are two elements of classic Greek drama. What other elements would you expect to see in a classic Greek stage play?

Russell Crowe

Skirts and sandals

Give the meaning of the term 'comic relief'.

It's that show with Lenny Henry and Pudsey the Bear.

Give an example of how movement can be used to show the personality of a character on stage.

If an actor moves around slowly it means they probably had a big meal before the play started.

Define the term ‘antagonist’.

Someone who tortures ants.

Give two examples of how an actor can convey emotion using their voice:

If they're trying to be funny they could speak in a squeaky voice.

Sketch an idea for a set design for *Who's Afraid of Virginia Woolf?*

As an actor playing the ghost in *Hamlet*, describe how you would use improvisation at a poignant moment in the play.

When it was my part I'd shout 'WOooOOooOOoooO!'

What is the function of the 'green room' in theatre production?

A garden area for the actors to smoke in.

Subject: English Language and Literature

Use the word 'pontificate' in a sentence to illustrate its meaning.

When you qualify as Pope, they give you a Pontificate.

Discuss one possible theme presented in the novella *The Picture of Dorian Gray.*

Making bad decisions:
If Dorian Gray had just used cosmetics none of that stuff would have happened and he'd still be OK.

Suggest an appropriate word for each of these meanings:

a) When a book is published after the author's death

b) An additional contest or period of play designed to establish a winner among tied contestants

c) When a person adds fictitious details or exaggerates facts or true stories

Prostate

Match-fixing

Embroidery

Write a sentence putting forward your own views on the subject of global warming.

IF THERE WAS GOING TO BE SOME SORT OF DISASTER IT WOULD BE GOOD TO LET EVERYONE KNOW, SO I AM FOR GLOBAL WARNINGS.

The following excerpt is from the poem 'I Wandered Lonely as a Cloud' by William Wordsworth.

I wandered lonely as a cloud
That floats on high o'er vales and hills,
When all at once I saw a crowd,
A host, of golden daffodils;
Beside the lake, beneath the trees,
Fluttering and dancing in the breeze.

Describe what the poet is feeling in this stanza.

I think the poet has taken
some drugs, because he thinks
he is a cloud and not a person.

In Harper Lee's novel *To Kill a Mockingbird*, what is the significance of Mrs Dubose?

She's the old person that nobody likes.

What is meant by the term 'non-fiction'?

It's the boring bit of the book shop that my grandad likes.

Consider the character of Jack in William Golding's *Lord of the Flies.* In what ways is he a strong leader?

He can climb up a whole beanstalk so he's probably pretty strong.

Give the term which best describes the highlighted section of the following sentence: The cat screeched **because the dog barked.**

The end.

Read the following poem by Christina Rossetti:

When I am dead, my dearest,
Sing no sad songs for me;
Plant thou no roses at my head,
Nor shady cypress tree:
Be the green grass above me
With showers and dewdrops wet;
And if thou wilt, remember,
And if thou wilt, forget.

In what ways does the poem make you feel sad?

It's not written in proper English.

Give one way in which George Orwell's *Animal Farm* explores political ideology.

Bacon is banned under communism.

Write the opening part of a speech intended to **persuade** pupils to stay in school.

I can't recommend school to anyone. I just go because my mum makes me.

Subject: Geography

Explain the ways in which intensive farming production can affect climate change.

The more burgers that are produced the more we can have barbecues and enjoy the extra sun.

Give some of the advantages and disadvantages of 'soft engineering' as a way of controlling flooding:

You can mould clay into lots of different shapes to build a barrier, but your hands get dirty.

Give one reason why deforestation happens in rainforests.

Rainforests are hot, so I don't think they get defrostation.

What are levees?

Expensive Jeans

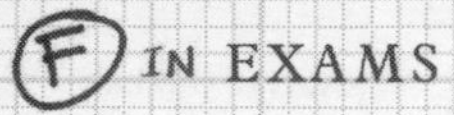

Satellites can be used to provide information for weather reports. Explain how.

There's no weather in space (apart from debris sometimes, like in the film Gravity).

Geography

Describe the differences between freeze-thaw weathering and chemical weathering.

Freeze-thaw weathering involves snow and hail, chemical weathering is just regular rain.

Explain how the rural-urban fringe around cities can be affected by expansion.

The fringe becomes shorter and makes the city look like it has a massive forehead.

Complete the following sentence:
Poorer countries generally have the CHEAPEST rates of population growth.

Give one advantage of living in a 'commuter village'.

Superfast broadband.

BLAST OFF!

Geography

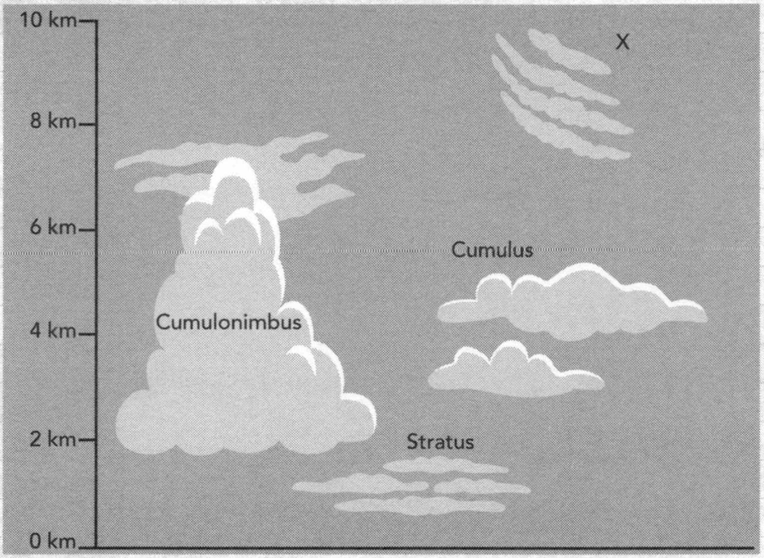

10 km
8 km
6 km
4 km
2 km
0 km
X
Cumulus
Cumulonimbus
Stratus

Name the cloud type at X.

Red arrows.

Give two ways in which governments of richer countries can cope with population growth:

Build a wall to stop more people coming into the country

By buying other countries to put the extra people in.

Outline one social impact of increased energy use.

Families get on better if everyone can use the internet at the same time.

Subject: History

Describe the role played by General MacArthur of the USA in the Korean War.

He played the role of an army general.

Give two examples of the medical knowledge that could be found in Ancient Egypt:

If bandages are put on too tightly they can suffocate people

Pointy houses prevent sunburn

Give reasons why Herbert Hoover lost the 1932 US Presidential election.

His new vacuum wasn't as good as the last one he invented.

Explain one effect of the Wall Street Crash in America in 1929.

A new wall had to be built.

The following symbol was conceived during the Russian Revolution in 1917.

What does is represent?

The Russian Gardening Club

Describe one way in which governments have controlled mass media in the twenty-first century.

Making us pay for TV licenses.

Why was George Stephenson important during the Industrial Revolution?

He wrote Treasure Island and Dr Jekyll and Mr Hyde.

Which figure in the British royal family is depicted above?

Dame Judy Dench.

THE GAP IN THE BRIDGE.

What does the following cartoon suggest about the League of Nations in 1920?

They were not very good builders.

Describe how Europe became divided by the Iron Curtain in the years 1945–1946.

When people started using iron curtains, some people liked them and some people didn't.

Use your own knowledge to explain why Winston Churchill was considered to be a good war leader.

He looked a bit like a bulldog, and a lot of people are scared of bulldogs.

Subject: Home Economics

Give examples of two food safety precautions which should be taken when preparing chicken for a pregnant woman:

Make sure you make it quick.

Make sure there are no feathers or anything on it, because you don't want to make the pregnant lady sick.

Describe ways in which a family on a low income can save money when buying food.

Don't bother with fancy things like vegetables.

Give examples of two foods which might cause allergies:

McDonald's fish burger and Turkish Delight. They both make me feel sick

Define the term 'functional foods'.

Functional foods are any foods that have a function, such as stopping you feeling hungry or giving you energy. So all foods.

Identify one of the main nutrients provided by each food group in the table below:

Food groups	Main nutrient
Bread, rice, potatoes	Dinner
Milk and dairy foods	Dessert
Meat, fish, eggs	Breakfast

Explain how food advice labels help the consumer.

Just looking at them makes them feel like they're more intelligent, even if they don't understand anything.

Give one example of how different protein foods can be combined to complement each other.

Fish and chips combine to make dinner on Friday Nights.

People can prevent food wastage by using up leftovers. The following table shows some typical household foods. In the spaces, write in how the leftover food might be used.

Leftover food	How it might be used
Pizza	Frisbee (only if it's whole)
Bread	Padding for the hole in the sofa
Potato	Paperweight

Suggest three factors to consider when buying a food processor:

Will it look nice in the kitchen?

Can I afford it?

Do I really need a food processor?

Give two nutrients which are **not found** in milk:

Beef and chicken.

Explain the chemical and physical differences between uncooked and cooked meat.

Uncooked meat ~~is~~ is uncooked.
Cooked meat is cooked.

Subject: ICT

What does the acronym OMR stand for?

Old monitor removal.

Describe one benefit of flash media.

Cool light effects.

Simon uses a desktop computer for gaming. His set-up includes a high-definition monitor, a keyboard, a mouse, speakers and a router. Give an example of another piece of related hardware which would enhance his gaming experience.

An X-box

Describe the impact of 3D printing on the manufacturing industry.

Instead of actually making things people can just print them.
It's quicker.

What function does the cc button have when sending an email?

IT BOOSTS THE SPEED OF THE EMAIL, LIKE WHEN A CAR HAS A BIGGER ENGINE WITH MORE CCs.

Describe a common way in which word processing software is used today.

Checking an essay's word count so you can think of the best way to pad it out.

What is meant by the term 'wiki'?

Information that you're not supposed to use for homework.

Computer microprocessors use cache memory. Give the meaning of 'cache memory'.

It's when your computer remembers all of the websites you spent money on.

State one possible effect on health from the use of monitors for computer work.

Better eyesight from staring at the screen so much.

Give one common way for a computer virus to get into a home computer system.

Sneezing on the screen.

Why is it necessary to use a browser to surf the internet?

They don't let you on it without one.

David and Sandra are parents of a child who attends nursery school. The nursery shares photographs of trips with parents as part of a photoblog. How might this be worrying for the parents?

The nursery might post an ugly photo of their kid.

Subject: Maths

David buys bananas at £6 per dozen (12) and sells them at 66p each.
What is his percentage profit?

100% from bananas

Simplify $\frac{y}{3} - \frac{y}{5}$

$$\frac{yy}{35}$$

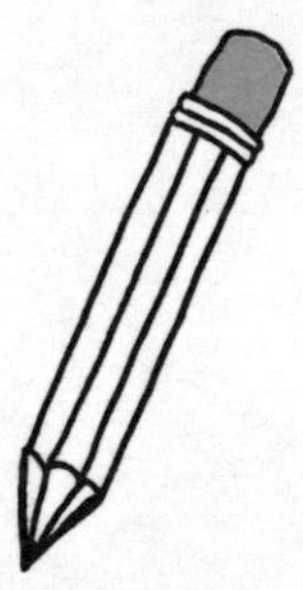

The Eurostar train leaves London at 10.32 (London time) and arrives in Paris at 13.45 (Paris time). The time in Paris is 1 hour ahead of the time in London. How long does the journey take?

Depends if it's before or after Brexit.

Write the number 40,000 in words.

Four zero zero zero zero.

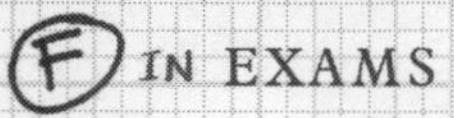

Purse A

Purse B

Purse A contains £10.20 in 10p coins.

Purse B contains only 5p coins.

The number of coins in purse B is three quarters of the number of coins in purse A.

How much money is in purse B?

That depends on how many coins are in the bag.

6x+1=19 can be best described as…

A secret code.

Robert estimates the answer to 32 × 49 is 1,500.
Show how he could have obtained this answer.

There are 1,000 people at a concert.

1/4 of the people are at stage 1.

1/3 of the people are at stage 2.

The rest are at stage 3.

How many people are at stage 3?

Depends on how close it is to the toilet, and if the band is any good.

Maths

What is the mathematical name of the shape below?

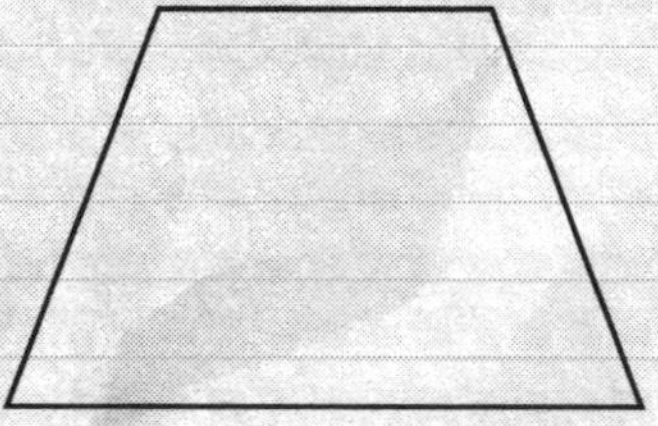

Irregular toblerone.

Complete the following sentence.

In data collection, the sum total of all numbers collected divided by the number of numbers is known as………

A job for a calculator

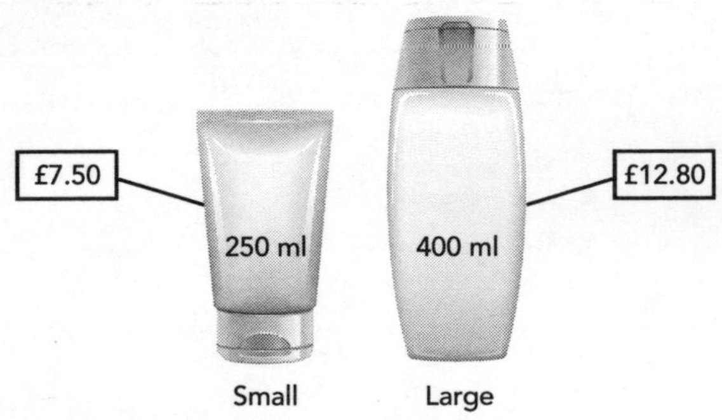

A pharmacy has two bestselling bottles of shampoo: one is 250 ml and the other is 400 ml.

Which is the better value for money?

They're both a waste of money if you have hair like mine.

Subject: Music

Describe what is meant by the term 'tonic chord'.

A chord that goes really well with a gin chord.

What group of instruments includes the helicon, mellophone and euphonium?

Transformers

Name two features that are typical of swing music:

Saxophones.

Old people.

Give the country of origin of the bouzouki.

I think it was invented by the American army.

Label at least three parts of this guitar:

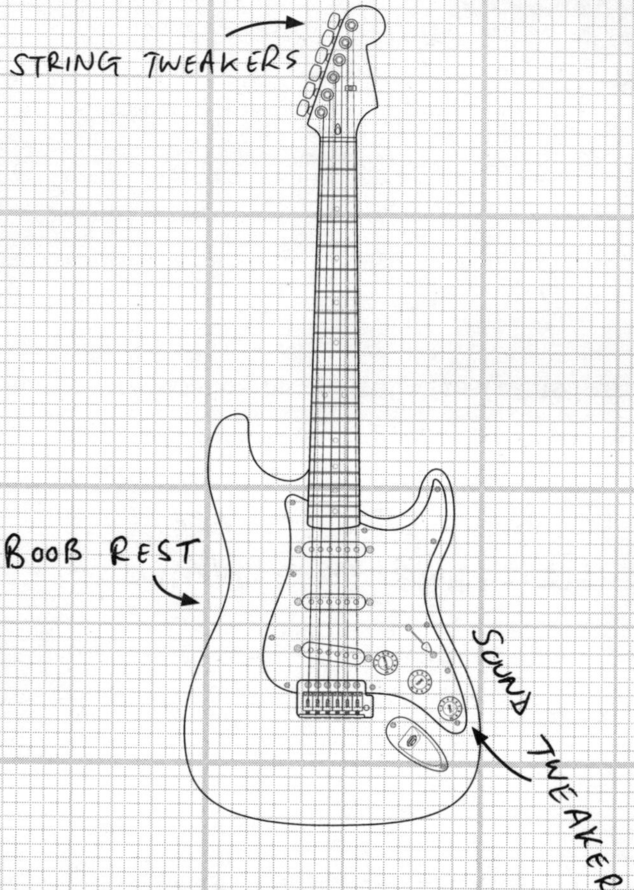

STRING TWEAKERS

BOOB REST

SOUND TWEAKERS

Define the term 'diminuendo'.

When you imply someone is stupid without actually saying it.

Give an example of musical styling in the music of The Beatles that would not be considered to be 'pop'.

Lyrics that don't make sense. People don't sit on cornflakes.

In what instance would you expect to hear an 'um cha-cha' rhythm?

In Willy Wonka's chocolate factory.

What word could be used to describe a group of four musicians playing together?

Buskers.

Music

What does the following group of symbols represent?

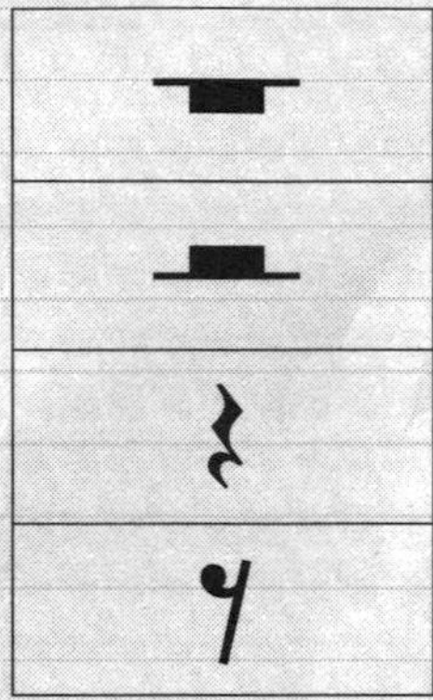

Types of hats worn by Lady Gaga.

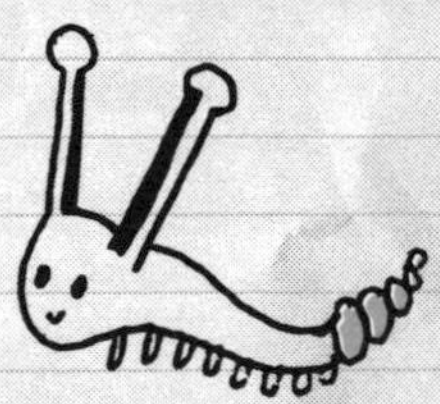

What kind of sounds would you expect to produce when striking the black keys on a piano or keyboard?

TING!

Describe the meaning of the term 'falsetto'.

When somebody sings the wrong note.

Subject: PE

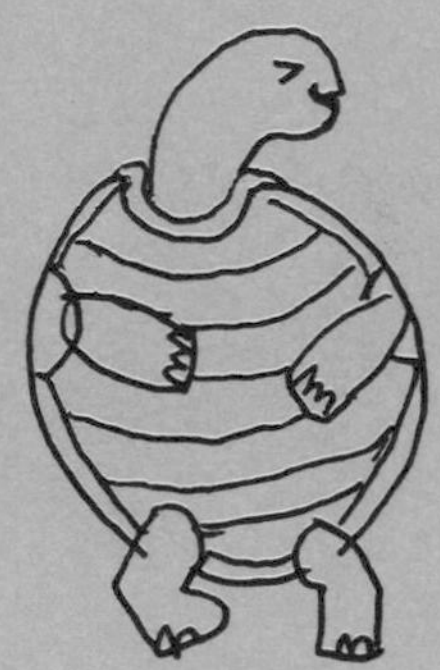

Explain the difference between isotonic and isometric exercise.

Isotonic exercise involves energy drinks, isometric exercise involves maths.

Give two reasons why endurance athletes should not consume tobacco products:

It's hard to smoke and run at the same time.

You shouldn't eat cigarettes - you smoke them

Name one aspect of fitness that could be tested by using the equipment pictured above.

Patience.

Give the meaning for each of the letters in the exercise acronym FITT:

Forget

It

Too

Tiring

The image above shows a gymnast performing a floor routine. Describe two physical qualities required to perform such a routine:

Double-jointedness

Clean underwear

Give an example of a sport which requires mostly anaerobic energy.

ANAEROBICS.

Give an example of a sport that would suit somebody with an ectomorph body type.

Shapeshifting.

State **two** things that a person might do in their lifestyle that would not help improve their physical health:

1. Get ill.

2. Waste hours looking at yoga pics on Instagram.

Give reasons why eating a large meal just before exercise might have a negative effect on performance:

You might need to use the toilet urgently.

You might have to burp loudly, which would be embarrassing.

Draw an arrow on the diagram below to show which part of the body a strained Achilles tendon would affect.

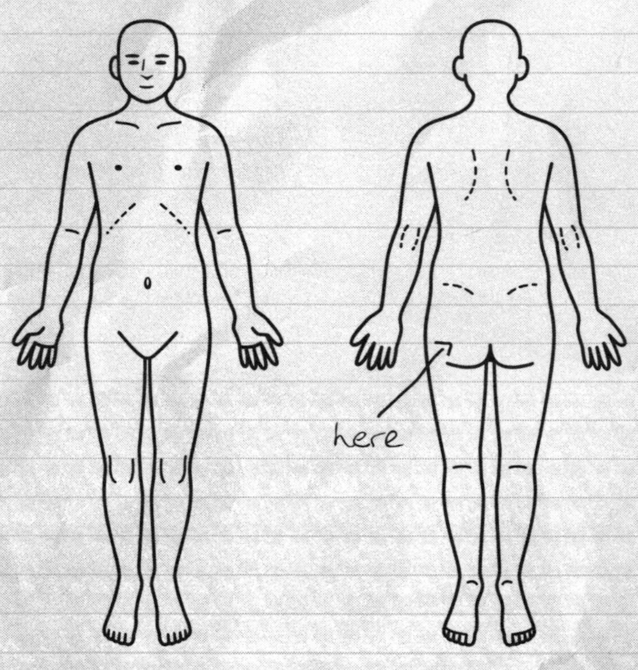

Lisa is regarded as an amateur gymnast. Explain what is meant by the term 'amateur'.

Amateur means you're not very good at the sport.

The image above shows a shot putter.
What key muscles are at work at this point in his action?

His face muscles. He looks very, very angry.

Subject: Religious Studies

Describe what is meant by the term ‘sacred’.

Cows.

Do you agree with the statement ‘Miracles never happen’? Explain your answer.

My mum always says
'Pigs might fly' and I've never
seen any, so I don't think
miracles can happen

Religious Studies

The image above shows the crucifixion of Jesus. Who is the woman depicted at Jesus' feet?

Madonna.

What does one religious tradition you have studied teach about Satan/the Devil?

Satanism teaches that the devil is cool

Explain why some people say sport has become a religion.

It's the only thing that can get my dad up on a Sunday.

What is meant by the term reincarnation?

It's when somebody gets sent back to jail after committing another crime.

Experiencing ghosts is evidence that people have spirits.
Do you agree or disagree? Explain your answer.

I've seen ghosts at Alton Towes and Drayton ~~P~~ Manor, so I think basecally only people who work in there parks have spirits.

What is meant by the term 'diversity'?

They are dancers who won the X Factor ages ago.

Religious Studies

Consider the statement 'Nature reveals the power of God.' Explain how God can be found in nature.

He goes there sometimes to get away from it all.

Explain why drinking alcohol is legal but using cannabis is illegal.

Eating people should never be legal.

Subject: Technology + Design

What does the following symbol signify?

You are part of the X-men team.

Describe the key difference between 'thermoplastic' and 'thermosetting' plastic.

The spelling.

The image above shows a notebook.
What term best describes the style of binding used?

Spaghetti

Give the definition for each of the letters in the acronym CAD:

C - Computer

A - Aided

D - Denial

Give two features of the city bicycle shown above which make it fit for its specific purpose:

The designer has given it wheels, which means it can roll along on the ground.

Trendy handlebars to make a statement.

Explain why you would screen print a T-shirt but not a park bench.

You might own a T-shirt but painting a park bench is vandalism.

Give the meaning of the term 'veneered finish'.

You've nearly finished something.

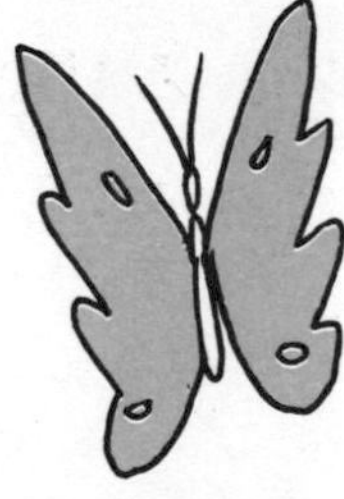

Give the meaning of the logo pictured above.

The circle of life.

Describe what you understand by the term 'nanotechnology'.

Nana technology is things like tea cosies and electric heaters.

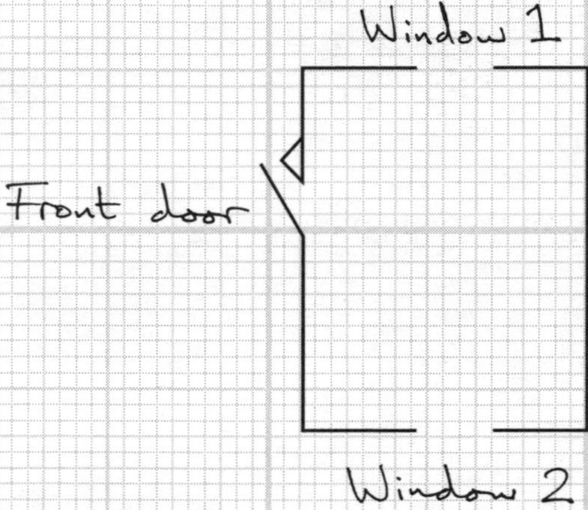

Add to the diagram above to show how it could function. Label your additions.

Subject: Business Studies and Economics

Explain what is meant when a business is described as 'organically grown'.

That business would sell fruit and vegetables.

In what instance would an anti-caking agent be used in food production?

It would be used by the government to stop people eating cakes. They would send out an anti-caking agent to stop people buying them.

Explain how the two documents described below can be used to select employees for a job.

1. Curriculum vitae (CV)
2. Application form

A CV with a nice photo will tell you if the person is attractive or not.

The application form will tell you if the person is an idiot or not.

Consumers regularly choose to buy counterfeit goods, rather than the genuine products. Should consumers be left to decide whether to buy counterfeit products, or should the government control the import and sale of these goods?

I don't think the government should be involved. They will just keep all the good stuff for themselves and not give us a chance to buy it.

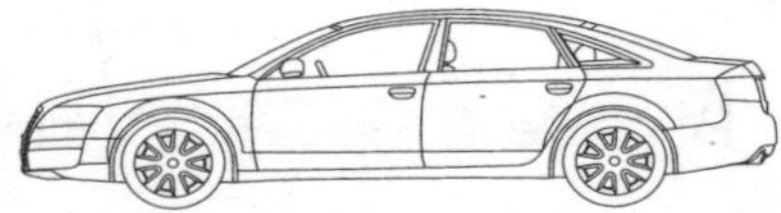

Explain two economic reasons why the price of second-hand cars might go down over the next few years.

The tyres will wear out, so it won't be worth as much.

It will lose the 'new car smell' which people pay for.

Explain what is meant by the term 'copyright'.

IT MEANS COPYING SOMETHING WITHOUT ANY MISTAKES.

Give two features of a matrix organisational structure:

Keanu Reeves is in charge.

The telephones are really good.

Agnes and Stephen run a business making and selling hats. There are several other businesses in the region who also sell hats.
Is Agnes and Stephen's business part of a competitive market or a monopoly?

A monopoly. There's definitely a hat in the game.

Explain what is meant by the the phrase 'division of labour'.

It's when the boss tells everybody else to work and then does nothing.

Claire has set up a new business selling plants. Explain one advantage and one disadvantage to Claire of using leaflets to advertise her business:

Advantage
Claire can get some exercise by putting them in everybody's letterbox.

Disadvantage
She will be tired from all of the running around.

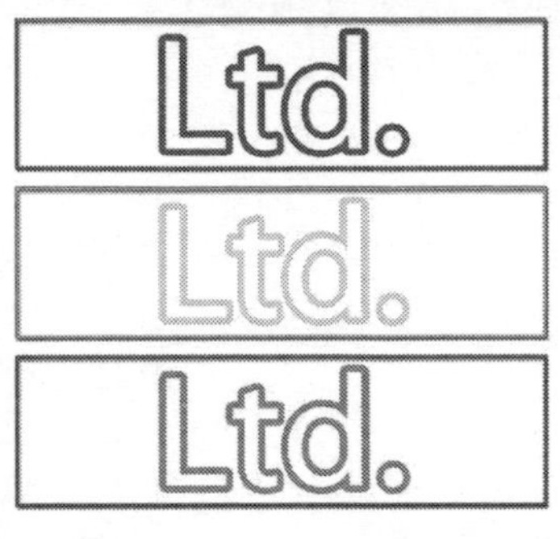

Give one feature of a private limited company.

It sells private limiteds.

Image credits (© Shutterstock)

p.9: HedgehogVector
p.10: panasbordin pimsin and AnutaBerg
p.14: Alona K
p.20: konstantinks
p.21: Michal Sanca
p.25: GzP_Design, petovarga, Demja and leosapiens
p.26: Lukas Bcran
p.29: PePI
p.30: Wstockstudio
p.34: LHF Graphics
p.42: maritime_m
p.45: RetroClipArt
p.50: 3Dsculptor
p.53: Nadya_Art
p.58: IndianSummer
p.60: Georgios Kollidas
p.69: Netkoff
p.74: dani3315
p.77: Ing. Andrej Kaprinay
p.82: Babiina
p.84: grynold
p.86: Kraska
p.90: vectorisland
p.97: Mikael Damkier
p.98: Lilyana Vynogradova
p.101: ankomando
p.102: Jamie Roach
p.105: jorisvo
p.106: Adrian Petyt
p.109: Oleg Belov
p.113: Vladislav Lyutov
p.114: Victor Metelskiy
p.116: Puntip Agitjarnrt
p.120: nasirkhan
p.121: galimovma79
p.123: vector-RGB
p.125: Friedrichan

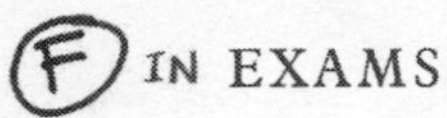

F IN EXAMS

The Big Book of
Test Paper Blunders

Richard Benson

£9.99

Hardback

ISBN:978-1-84953-924-1

Exams have never been so hilarious!

Banish the horror of school days with this bumper edition of the world's ~~worst~~ best test paper blunders. Bursting with misunderstandings, misspellings and spirited – if ultimately incorrect – answers, this collection brings together the most head-scratching, side-splitting examples from the *F in Exams* series.

If you're interested in finding out more about our books, find us on Facebook at **Summersdale Publishers** and follow us on Twitter at **@Summersdale**.

www.summersdale.com